Lovely
LABRADOR
RETRIEVERS

GENTLE! LOYAL! LOVING!

FRIENDLY! DEVOTED! KEEN!

ABDO
Publishing Company

Pam Scheunemann

Consulting Editor, Diane Craig, M.A./Reading Specialist

Published by ABDO Publishing Company
8000 West 78th Street, Edina, Minnesota 55439.

Printed in the United States.

Editor: Pam Price
Content Developer: Nancy Tuminelly
Cover and Interior Design and Production:
    Anders Hanson, Mighty Media
Illustrations: Bob Doucet
Photo Credits: Shutterstock

Library of Congress Cataloging-in-Publication Data

Scheunemann, Pam, 1955-
 Lovely labrador retrievers / Pam Scheunemann ; illustrated by
Bob Doucet.
   p. cm. -- (Dog daze)
 ISBN 978-1-60453-618-8
 1. Labrador retriever--Juvenile literature. I. Doucet, Bob. II. Title.

SF429.L3S33 2009
636.752'7--dc22

                      2008040267

Super SandCastle™ books are created by a team of
professional educators, reading specialists, and content
developers around five essential components—phonemic
awareness, phonics, vocabulary, text comprehension, and
fluency—to assist young readers as they develop reading
skills and strategies and increase their general
knowledge. All books are written, reviewed, and leveled
for guided reading, early reading intervention, and
Accelerated Reader® programs for use in shared, guided,
and independent reading and writing activities to support
a balanced approach to literacy instruction.

CONTENTS

The LABRADOR RETRIEVER

Labrador retrievers are hardworking, **loyal**, friendly dogs. As their name says, they are great at retrieving. They were **bred** as hunting dogs. But they also make nice working dogs or family pets.

Labrador retrievers are also called Labs.

FACIAL FEATURES

Head

Labrador retrievers have broad heads.

Teeth and Mouth

The Labrador retriever's jaws are powerful.

Eyes

The eyes of the Labrador retriever are usually brown or hazel.

Ears

Labrador retrievers have floppy ears. They hang close to the head.

4

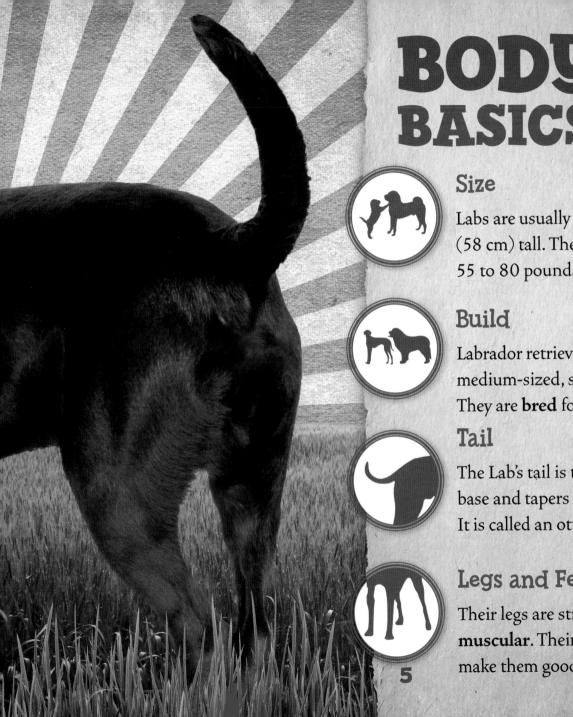

BODY BASICS

Size

Labs are usually about 23 inches (58 cm) tall. They can weigh from 55 to 80 pounds (25 to 36 kg).

Build

Labrador retrievers are medium-sized, sturdy dogs. They are **bred** for hunting.

Tail

The Lab's tail is thick at the base and tapers to a point. It is called an otter tail.

Legs and Feet

Their legs are strong and **muscular**. Their webbed feet make them good swimmers.

COAT & COLOR

Labrador Retriever Fur

The coat of the Labrador retriever is short, straight, and dense. The soft undercoat provides protection from cold and water.

The coat colors are black, yellow, and chocolate. Blacks are all black. Yellows can range from fox-red to light cream. Chocolates can vary from light to dark brown.

YELLOW PUPPY

CHOCOLATE PUPPY

BLACK PUPPY

YELLOW FUR

CHOCOLATE FUR

BLACK FUR

YELLOW ADULT

CHOCOLATE ADULT

BLACK ADULT

HEALTH & CARE

Life Span

The **life span** of the Labrador retriever is 10 to 12 years.

Grooming

Labs tend to shed a little every day. During the spring and the fall, they will shed more heavily. Labs need regular grooming. Brush their coats weekly.

VET'S CHECKLIST

- Have your Labrador retriever spayed or neutered.

- Do not let your Labrador retriever overeat.

- Visit a vet for regular checkups.

- Ask your vet which foods are right for your Lab.

- Clean your Lab's teeth and ears once a week.

- Make sure your Labrador retriever gets a lot of exercise.

EXERCISE & TRAINING

Activity Level

Labrador retrievers have an average activity level. They need regular exercise and interesting things to do. If they cannot vent their energy, they will become bored. They can become **destructive** when they are bored.

Obedience

Labs are independent, but they respond well to obedience training. Some may have a stubborn streak.

A Few Things You'll Need

A **leash** lets your Lab know that you are the boss. With a leash, you can guide your dog where you want it to go. Most cities require that dogs be on leashes when they are outside.

A **collar** is a strap that goes around your Lab's neck. You can attach a leash to the collar to take your dog on walks. You should also attach an **identification tag** with your home address. If your dog ever gets lost, people will know where it lives.

Toys keep your Lab healthy and happy. Labs like to chase and chew on toys.

A **dog bed** will help your pet feel safe and comfortable at night.

ATTITUDE & INTELLIGENCE

Personality

Labrador retrievers are loving and **loyal**. They have a high energy level and like to please. They need to be properly trained.

Intellect

Labs are smart dogs. Many of them are working dogs, such as **service dogs** and police dogs.

All About Me

Hi! My name is Lucky. I'm a Lab. I just wanted to let you know a few things about me. I made some lists below of things I like and dislike. Check them out!

Things I Like

- Lots of exercise
- Showing my excitement
- Playing fetch
- Chewing things
- Swimming
- Hunting

Things I Dislike

- Being ignored
- Being left alone
- Boredom
- Not getting enough exercise

LITTERS & PUPPIES

Litter Size

Female Labrador retrievers usually give birth to seven or eight puppies.

Diet

Newborn pups drink their mother's milk. Labs can begin to eat soft puppy food when they are about five weeks old.

Growth

They should stay with their mothers until they are eight weeks old. Labrador retriever puppies grow until they are about three years old.

BUYING A LAB

Choosing a Breeder

It's best to buy a puppy from a **breeder**, not a pet store. When you visit a dog breeder, ask to see the mother and father of the puppies. Make sure the parents are healthy, friendly, and well behaved.

Picking a Puppy

Choose a puppy that isn't too **aggressive** or too shy. If you crouch down, some of the puppies may want to play with you. One of them might be the right one for you!

Is It the Right Dog for You?

Buying a dog is a big decision. You'll want to make sure your new pet suits your lifestyle.

Get out a piece of paper. Draw a line down the middle.

Read the statements listed here. Each time you agree with a statement from the left column, make a mark on the left side of your paper. When you agree with a statement from the right column, make a mark on the right side of your paper.

I like to play with my dog.	☐	☐	I want my dog to entertain itself.
I want to work on training my dog.	☐	☐	I don't want to train my dog.
I like a dog that gets along with other dogs.	☐	☐	I don't care if my dog gets along with other dogs.
I spend a lot of time at home.	☐	☐	I'm not home very often.
I like to teach my dog tricks.	☐	☐	I don't want to teach my dog tricks.
I like to play fetch with my dog.	☐	☐	I don't like to play fetch with my dog.
I like a big dog.	☐	☐	I prefer a small lapdog.

If you made more marks on the left side than on the right side, a Lab may be the right dog for you! If you made more marks on the right side of your paper, you might want to consider another breed.

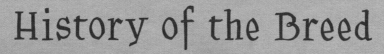

History of the Breed
THE FRIENDLY WORKING DOG

Labrador retrievers originated on an island near Labrador, Canada. The dogs were noted for their retrieving abilities and good nature. They would work with the fishermen during the day and then play with the fishermen's children at night.

In the early 1800s, some of these dogs were exported to England. At that time, several **breeders** in England were developing different types of retrievers. It is said that one of the breeders, the Earl of Malmesbury, was the first to call them Labradors.

19

Tails of Lore
A REMARKABLE RETRIEVER

Endal is a special Labrador retriever that lives in England. Endal is a helper and therapy dog for Allen Parton. Allen uses a wheelchair to get around, and Endal helps him do a lot of everyday tasks.

20

Labrador retrievers make great **canine** partners. Endal understands voice and hand signals. He helps Allen do the laundry and make dinner. He even helps out at the cash machine! Allen and Endal have a true partnership.

FIND THE LAB

A   B   C   D

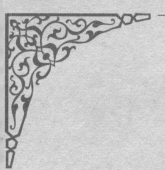

THE LAB QUIZ

1. Labrador retrievers have powerful jaws. **True or false?**

2. Labrador retrievers are not good swimmers. **True or false?**

3. Labs don't shed every day. **True or false?**

4. Labrador retrievers need a lot of exercise. **True or false?**

5. Labrador retrievers can be police dogs. **True or false?**

6. Labrador retrievers make great canine partners. **True or false?**

GLOSSARY

aggressive – likely to attack or confront.

breed – 1) a group of animals or plants with common ancestors. 2) to raise animals, such as dogs or cats, that have certain traits. A *breeder* is someone whose job is to breed certain animals or plants.

canine – having to do with dogs.

destructive – causing damage.

life span – the average length of time someone or something exists.

loyal – faithful or devoted to someone or something.

muscular – having well-developed muscles.

service dog – a dog trained to assist people who have disabilities.

About SUPER SANDCASTLE™

Bigger Books for Emerging Readers
Grades K–4

Created for library, classroom, and at-home use, Super SandCastle™ books support and engage young readers as they develop and build literacy skills and will increase their general knowledge about the world around them. Super SandCastle™ books are part of SandCastle™, the leading preK–3 imprint for emerging and beginning readers. Super SandCastle™ features a larger trim size for more reading fun.

Let Us Know

Super SandCastle™ would like to hear your stories about reading this book. What was your favorite page? Was there something hard that you needed help with? Share the ups and downs of learning to read. We want to hear from you! Send us an e-mail.

sandcastle@abdopublishing.com

Contact us for a complete list of SandCastle™, Super SandCastle™, and other nonfiction and fiction titles from ABDO Publishing Company.

www.abdopublishing.com • 8000 West 78th Street
Edina, MN 55439 • 800-800-1312 • 952-831-1632 fax